The Ladies' Aid Society

The Universal Cook Book

The Ladies' Aid Society

The Universal Cook Book

ISBN/EAN: 9783744792455

Printed in Europe, USA, Canada, Australia, Japan

Cover: Foto ©Andreas Hilbeck / pixelio.de

More available books at **www.hansebooks.com**

THE

UNIVERSAL COOK BOOK

PUBLISHED BY

THE LADIES' AID SOCIETY

OF . .

THE FIRST UNIVERSALIST CHURCH.

. OF .

ENGLEWOOD,

CHICAGO:
STEWART AVENUE AND SIXTY-FIFTH STREET
COPYRIGHTED 1891.

SOUPS

FISH

OYSTERS, ETC.

MEATS

VEAL

MUTTON AND LAMB

PORK

POULTRY

VEGETABLES

EGGS

WELSH RARE

SALADS

BREAD, BREAKFAST CAKES, ETC.

PASTRY

CAKES

PRESERVES AND PICKLES

PUDDINGS AND DESSERTS

INTRODUCTORY.

In offering to the public this first edition of the "UNIVERSAL COOK BOOK" the ladies in charge of its publication desire to return their thanks to the many firms whose advertising patronage has assured success to the enterprise.

We believe we can conscientiously recommend every article found advertised herein.

We gratefully acknowledge a generous donation of Evaporated Cream and delicious Ice Cream from the Helvetia Milk Condensing Co.; a quantity of "New England" Condensed Mince Meat from the manufacturer, T. E. Dougherty, and an elegant silver "Self Pouring" Teapot from Paine, Diehl & Co., of Philadelphia.

Attention is called to the CAN OPENER advertised by Boothby & Co. It is a time and temper saver and renders can opening no longer an unpleasant task.

Our obligations extend to the King's Daughters of Provincetown, Mass., who have kindly supplied many excellent recipes from their own cook book.

Especial care has been observed in the selection of recipes, all of which have been closely scanned and revised by the members of Mrs. Riley's cooking class who have also added a large number of new an valuable formulas.

We have endeavored to compile a useful, practical, "every day" cook book and with confidence in its merits we submit the result of our efforts.

THE LADIES' AID SOCIETY.

Englewood Universalist Church.

FIRST UNIVERSALIST CHURCH,

Stewart Ave. & 65th St., Englewood,
CHICAGO.

Sunday Services, 10:30 a. m.
Young People's Meeting, 7:00 p. m.
Sunday School, 12:10 p. m.

STRANGERS

CORDIALLY

INVITED.

Pastor.
FLORENCE E. KOLLOCK,   6565 Harvard Street.

Trustees.
JOHN W. MOORE, PRESIDENT,   6510 Yale Street.
MRS. E. W. TRUE, SECRETARY,   323 Sixty-first St.
G. W. CARSON,   J. A. STODDARD.
A. J. HOAGLAND,   J. F. OLMSTEAD,
W. M. BROWN,   E. A. RICE,   W. W. CARTER.

Secretary.
S. S. WILLARD.   6552 Perry Ave.

Treasurer.
W. S. WOOD,   6638 LaFayette Avenue.

Sunday School.
Ashleigh C. Halliwell, Superintendent.   Mrs. S. E. Jennings, Vice-Superintendent.
S. C. Mason, Secretary.   Miss Kittie Baldwin, Asst. Secretary.
H. P. Ludden, Treasurer.   Col. Francis W. Parker, Senior Bible Class.

Ladies' Aid Society.
Mrs. J. S. Osgood, President.   Mrs. F. Salter, Mrs. A. W. Todd, Mrs. Ervin A. Rice, Vice-
Presidents.
Mrs D. W. Miller, Secretary.   Mrs. W. S. Wood, Treasurer.

Young People's Christian Union.
Fred Guthrie, President.   Emma Brown, Vice-President.   Rufus Scott, Secretary.
Grace Monroe, Treasurer.

King's Daughters.
Belle Brayton, President.   Maggie Weir, Vice-President.   Carrie Jennings, Secretary.
Lillan Dean, Treas.   Mrs. Osgood, Miss Hoagland, Miss Brown, Directors.

... THE ...

Universal Cook Book.

SOUPS.

STOCK I.

Take six pounds of shin of beef; wipe it and cut meat from the bone into small pieces; put bone and part of meat into a kettle and cover with four quarts of cold water. Let it soak a half hour. Take marrow which was cut from meat and melt in a pan. Slice three onions and fry brown in marrow, skim into the kettle and put in remaining meat and fry brown; add this to soup, then three tablespoons each of carrot and turnips, two stalks celery, little parsley and bayleaf, ten cloves, ten pepper corns and three teaspoons mixed herbs, tied in a cloth. One tablespoon salt. Simmer eight or ten hours and strain. Cool quickly. Remove the fat, allow white and shell of one egg for each quart of stock. Beat egg and mix well with cold stock. Then heat and boil five minutes. Remove, add one-half cup cold water and let it stand until ready to strain. Strain through napkin or double cheese cloth laid over fine strainer.

STOCK 2.

Procure a shin of beef. Have it broken in parts, let it boil slowly at the back of the range all day in a gallon of water; at night skim out the bones and meat, and set the soup away in a cool place, closely covered. Next morning you will have a thick jelly covered with fat which should be skimmed off, leaving a fine base for soup, which may be weakened if preferred. If not, add for soup an onion and a piece of butter, size of an egg, which have been browned in same pan, a tablespoonful of browned flour, mixed with a teaspoonful of celery salt, and a tablespoonful of Worchestershire sauce; cut up a carrot, a turnip, a root of celery, a little parsley, thyme or summer savory, and to all add a few cloves (half a dozen) and pepper to taste. Add all and let them cook till the vegetables are done. Then strain and serve.

SAVE THE BONES FOR SOUP.

Many housekeepers throw away the stock for good soups. You should save the scraps of beefsteak and the bones of a roast. Two or three kinds make it all the better. The carcass of a turkey or a pair of fowls make excellent soup with rice or barley. Boil the bones for five or six hours, let stand over night, then remove the fat and strain. Any kind of soup can be made by adding tomato, vermicelli, macaroni or chopped vegetables.

SOUPS.

All vegetables are available for soup. The favorite vegetable soup made from fresh tomatoes, corn and Lima beans is almost as good when the canned vegetables are employed. For chicken soup with rice and milk, no herbs but parsley should be used. The shin of veal or beef is the legitimate soup-bone; but any other bone may be used. Crack the bones before boiling, for the sake of the marrow, and do not put salt in until the meat has been well boiled—it has a tendency to harden the fibers and prevent the flow of the juices of the meat. You cannot well boil it too long, short of the time when the meat boils into rags and strings. If kept where they will not sour, and heated slowly so as not to scorch, most soups are better the second day than the first.

VEAL SOUP WITH SPAGHETTI.

Three pounds veal, knuckle or scrag, with the bones broken, and meat cut off, three quarts water, one-fourth pound spaghetti. Boil the meat in the water alone until reduced to shreds, three hours at least. Cook the spaghetti, broken into inch pieces, in water, in a vessel by itself, till tender. Add a little butter to the spaghetti, just as it is done; strain the meat out of its soup; season to taste; put in the spaghetti and the water it was cooked in. Let it boil up once and serve.

CONSOMME.

Five pounds of clear beef cut from the lower part of the round, five quarts cold water; cut the beef into small pieces, add the water and let it come to a boil gradually; skim carefully and set where it will keep at the boiling point eight or ten hours; strain and set away to cool. In the morning skim off all the fat, pour the soup into a kettle, being careful to keep back the sediment. Put into the soup one onion, one stalk of celery, two sprigs of parsley, two sprigs of thyme, two of summer savory, two leaves of sage, two bay leaves, twelve pepper corns, six whole cloves; boil gently twenty minutes, strain through a napkin, first seasoning with salt and pepper to taste; tie the herbs together before putting into the soup.

BOUILLON.

Two pounds lean beef chopped fine, pour over it one quart cold water, put it in a porcelain kettle, cover tight and let it simmer four hours. Strain off the tea and let it cool, beat the white of one egg and add to the tea, put it on the stove and stir until it comes to a boil; let it boil until it becomes perfectly clear, skimming, then strain through a fine napkin and season with salt to taste.

POTATO SOUP.

Three pints of rich milk, one pint of mashed potato, two tablespoonfuls of butter, pepper and salt to taste. Boil the milk, add the potato and boil again, stirring frequently that the potato may become thoroughly dissolved, and season just before serving, Serve very hot.

ONION SOUP.

Three pints of milk in which six good-sized onions have been boiled makes a delicious soup, seasoned to taste with butter, salt and pepper, thickened, with two tablespoonfuls of flour made smooth in cold milk. Onions are much nicer boiled in milk than in water.

CORN SOUP.

Eight large ears; cut off the grains and scrape well the cob; cover it with water; boil until perfectly well done. Be careful not to put too much water with it. Add two quarts of milk; let it come to a boil; stir in two tablespoonfuls of butter rolled in two tablespoonfuls of flour; let it boil for 10 minutes. Pour the soup on the yolks of three eggs well beaten, and serve.

TOMATO SOUP.

Stew one half can tomatoes until soft, and strain. If very sour add one half teaspoonful soda, then one quart of Stock 1. before it is cleared; one teaspoonful sugar, salt and pepper to taste. If desired thicken with one tablespoon each of flour and butter cooked together.

Butter slices of stale bread, cut in small squares, place in tin pan butter side up and brown in a quick oven. Serve with the soup.

TOMATO SOUP WITH MILK.

Four very large tomatoes cut up fine; or one can of tomatoes; put on the stove with one quart of water and let this come to a boil and add one even teaspoonful of soda dissolved in water. Boil three quarters of an hour and add one pint of milk, also pepper, salt and butter. When this boils, thicken with cracker dust and serve.

BISQUE OF TOMATOES.

To one quart of tomatoes, add one quart of water, one small onion, twelve cloves; boil one hour; strain; add piece of butter size of an egg; salt and pepper to taste; one teaspoon corn starch dissolved in a little milk, one half teaspoon of soda dissolved in a little water. Scald one quart of milk and add just before serving.

Do you eat bread? ❋ ❋ ❋

If you do, then you are interested in having only the BEST FLOUR. This can be secured of any first-class grocer by asking for

Washburn's . . . Superlative Flour

Made in the famous

Washburn Mills, ❋ ❋

❋ ❋ Minneapolis, Minn.

DAILY CAPACITY 9,000 BARRELS.

Only the Choicest MINNESOTA and DAKOTA wheat is used in the manufacture of our SUPERLATIVE FLOUR. To get the GENUINE **Washburn Mills Flour** see that our firm name *in full* is on each barrel or sack.

WASHBURN CROSBY CO.

OYSTER SOUP.

Pour one pint of water on one quart oysters, stir well and take out singly with the fingers and drain in colander. Strain, heat and skim the liquor, add another pint of water or milk, season with two teaspoons of salt and pepper. When boiling add oysters, stir gently and when ready to boil again, remove and serve.

BISQUE OF OYSTERS.

One quart oysters, one quart cream, one pint chicken stock, if you don't have it use water. One scant pint stale bread free of crust, one bay leaf, one sprig of parsley, one stalk of celery, one small slice of onion, a bit of whole mace, two tablespoons of butter, one tablespoon flour, yolks of four eggs, pepper and salt to taste.

Wash and chop the oysters, strain, heat and skim the liquid. After skimming add one half the chicken stock or water, the oysters and seasoning. Simmer twenty minutes; cook bread and rest of chicken stock or water until soft. Strain the first saucepan into the bread pressing all juice out of oysters then strain it back again. Keep one half cup of cream, put the remainder into double boiler to heat, then add two tablespoons of flour and two of butter cooked together. Then add the first mixture and just before serving add the yolks of two eggs well beaten with the half cup of cream. The soup may be prepared some time in advance and then kept over hot water until wanted, when the egg and cream should be added.

PUREE OF SALMON.

Remove oil. bone and skin from one half can salmon. Chop fish very fine. Cook one slice onion in one quart milk ten minutes or more. Remove onion and thicken milk with one tablespoon each of butter and flour cooked together. Season with one teaspoon of salt, one saltspoon pepper add salmon; when hot serve.

CHICKEN BROTH.

Clean the chicken and separate it at the joints. Remove all the skin and fat. Cover the chicken with cold water. Add one tablespoonful of salt, one saltspoonful of pepper, one small onion, sliced. Simmer until the

chicken is tender. Remove the best part of the meat, and put the bones
and gristle back and simmer until the bones are clean. Strain the broth.
Remove the fat. Put the broth on to boil again and add to it the rice
which has been thoroughly washed and soaked in cold water, and the nic-
est portions of meat cut into small pieces. Simmer until the rice is tender.
Add seasoning to taste, and serve at once.

FISH.

—

TO BOIL SALMON.

Allow twenty minutes for boiling every pound. Wrap it in a floured
cloth and lay it in the kettle. Make the water very salt. Skim it well.
Serve it with drawn butter or egg sauce.

SALMON LOAF.

Extract the bones from the contents of one can of salmon, and rub to
a paste with two large spoons of soft butter. Add two-thirds of a cup of
crumbs moistened with half a cup of milk. Season with salt, pepper and
lemon juice. Add last four beaten eggs. Place in well buttered quart
mould or pan, cover and steam one hour. Turn out on platter and pour
sauce around made as follows: Let one large cup of milk come to a boil,
then thicken with one tablespoon of corn starch dissolved in a little milk;
add one tablespoon of butter and season with salt and pepper. Add a beat-
en egg last. Garnish the edge of the platter with lemon, or parsley.

FISH TURBOT.

Arrange cold fish (either white or trout) broken into flakes, in layers in a buttered dish with crumbs, hard boiled egg and milk gravy, using butter, pepper and salt. Cover with crumbs and bake in moderate oven half an hour.

BAKED WHITE FISH.

Split a good sized white fish and extract back-bone; lay in a buttered dripping pan with skin down, dredge well with flour, add lumps of butter, season and pour half a cup of water in the pan; bake about forty minutes in moderate oven.

SALMON ON TOAST.

Heat thoroughly the contents of a can of salmon; prepare one and one-half cups of milk gravy, break fish in flakes and place neatly on slices of toast, sprinkle with lemon juice, cover with gravy and serve.

STUFFED AND BAKED TROUT.

Make stuffing with one cup of cracker crumbs, one-third cup of melted butter, salt, pepper and a teaspoon each of chopped onion, parsley, capers and pickles. Moisten a little with warm water. After cleaning the fish, wash and wipe well; stuff and sew up. If narrow, skewer in shape of S and fasten skewers in, then place on fish sheet. Rub all over with salt, pepper and butter. Cut gashes two inches apart in fish and put in narrow strips of fat salt pork. Dredge with flour and place in oven. When flour browns add water and baste occasionally. It should bake an hour or more and must be removed carefully to a platter well heated; the pork and skewers removed and sauce poured around it.

Hollandaise Sauce.—Cream half a cup of butter, add one teaspoon of flour and yolks of two eggs singly, when smooth add salt, cayenne pepper and lemon juice gradually. Before serving add half a cup of boiling water and stir over water until thickened.

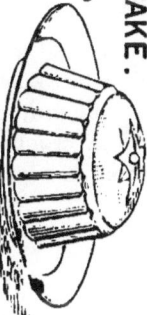

FISH CHOWDER.

Take two pounds of haddock or cod, and cut in two inch cubes, and also an equal amount of potatoes in thin slices. Soak potatoes in cold water then place in boiling water for five minutes, and drain. Cut a two inch cube of fat salt pork into dice and fry in a pan; slice a large onion thin and fry in pork fat. Pour fat through a strainer into a kettle, put in potatoes and cover with boiling water. When boiling again add fish and seasoning and simmer fifteen minutes, then add a tablespoon of butter and a quart of hot milk. Place six split butter crackers in a tureen and pour chowder over.

TURBANS OF FISH.

Fillet two fish and season pieces with salt, pepper and lemon juice and put in cool place half an hour or more, then dip them in melted butter, roll in fine crumbs, egg beaten with water, and crumbs again. Roll these up and fasten each with a tooth-pick. Fry in hot deep lard until brown and serve with tartare sauce.

Tartare Sauce.—To mayonnaise or other salad dressing add chopped pickles. olives, capers, parsley, one or all.

FISH CROQUETTES.

Take equal amount of cold flaked fish and white sauce made in proportions of 2 spoons each of butter and flour to one pint of milk. Season with lemon juice and salt and pepper. Shape in croquettes, roll in egg, crumbs, and egg again and fry brown in smoking hot lard.

FISH BALLS.

Soak half a pound of codfish over night. Place on the stove in cold water in the morning, let it come to a boil, remove and drain. Pick it over, remove bones and chop fine. Then add a pint of hot mashed potatoes, and a well beaten egg. Mix thoroughly, form into balls and fry in part pork fat and part lard.

OYSTERS.

—

PLAIN OYSTER STEW.

Take one pint oysters, add half cup cold water, stir with fork. Take out of liquor with fork, one at a time; put in a sauce pan with part of the liquor strained through fine sieve; put on the stove and when it comes to a boil, add one quart milk and skim carefully. Let it come to a boil again but do not boil, add salt to taste, one third cup butter and stir until butter is all dissolved; serve.

OYSTER CUTLETS.

Soak two tablespoons of bread crumbs in liquor from one cup of oysters. Chop oysters fine and add crumbs, one cup chopped chicken and salt, pepper and lemon juice. Cook one tablespoon each of flour and butter until frothy, add the oyster mixture and cook three minutes; add two well beaten eggs and stir until it thickens. Spread on a platter to cool; then butter cutlet mould well, dip in crumbs, fill with oyster mixture, drop into crumbs, and repeat until all are formed. Then dip in one beaten egg with one tablespoon of water, and in crumbs again. Fry in smoking hot lard until brown.

FRIED OYSTERS.

Open the oysters and put them in a colander for about half an hour. They must be as well drained as possible. Then dip them in egg and roll in bread crumbs in the following way: Beat one or two or three eggs (according to the quantity of oysters to be fried), as for an omelet, turn

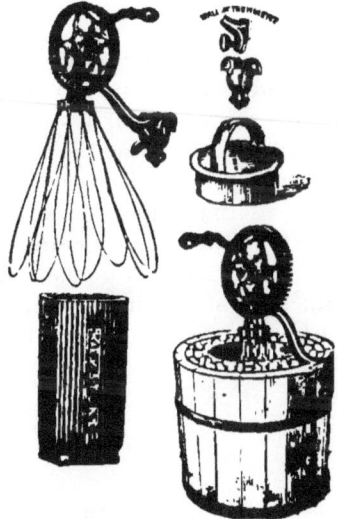

the oysters into the eggs and stir gently; then take one after another, roll in bread crumbs; place each one in your left hand, in taking them from the crumbs, and with the other hand press gently on it. Put them away in a cool place for about half an hour, and then dip again in egg; roll in bread crumbs and press in the hand as before. While you are preparing them set some fat on the fire in a pan, and when hot enough drop the oysters in, stir gently, take off with a skimmer when fried, turn into a colander, add salt, and serve hot.

ESCALOPED OYSTERS.

Butter the sides and bottom of the baking dish. Examine the oysters carefully and remove any pieces of shell; then cover the bottom of the dish with a thick layer of oysters, put lumps of butter thickly over the top and sprinkle with salt and pepper. Next lay a layer, not too deep, of bread crumbs and pounded crackers, half and half. Fill the dish in this manner with alternate layers of oysters, seasoning, bread and cracker crumbs, covering the top with crumbs and lumps of butter. Do not add liquid of any kind, and if there has not been too large a proportion of bread and cracker used it will be sufficiently moist, and will be much better made in this way. One-half hour at least will be required in baking.

OYSTER CHOWDER.

Wash one quart oysters, pick over, drain and boil the oyster liquor; skim; cut a one-inch cube of salt pork into small pieces and fry; fry one onion cut fine in the pork fat until yellow; skim out the scraps of pork and onion, and put in three-fourths of a quart of pared and sliced potatoes which have been parboiled; cover with boiling water and cook until tender then add the oyster liquor and the oysters; cook until their edges curl; add two tablespoonfuls flour, moistened with a little cold water until a thin paste; cook five minutes; add one pint hot milk, one tablespoonful butter, salt and pepper to taste; add a few oyster crackers and serve. The onion and pork may be omitted from the above rule if desired. The potatoes are parboiled to extract any bitter taste they may have. The thickening can be omitted if preferred.

STUFFED OYSTERS.

Hash and drain on several thicknesses of cloth some large oysters. Season with salt, pepper and lemon juice. Make a forcemeat by chopping a quarter of a pound of raw veal, then rub through a sieve. Cook a quarter of a cup of stale bread with half a cup of cream until smooth, add meat and cook a minute, remove and add salt, pepper and lemon juice, and beaten white of one egg. Mix well and when cool spread on half of the oysters. Lay on the other half and press together. Season fine crumbs with salt and pepper, roll oysters in them then egg and crumbs again. Fry in lard.

OYSTER PATTIES.

Make a dozen shells of rich puff paste. Prepare oysters by making a pint of rich sauce with part cream. Season this and add oyster liquor from a pint of oysters. Then add oysters and cook until plump. When ready to serve pour into heated shells.

Delicious and Refreshing

"Say, Mama, I want another glass of
'Hires' Root Beer.'"

Hires' Root Beer

Makes the purest and most delicious drink in the world. Sparkling and appetizing. An article of real merit and genuine worth, commanding attention by its intrinsic value, purifying the blood, cleansing the system of poisonous humors, and making a clear, rosy complexion.

Do not be put off by dealers telling you that some other kind is just as good. Insist upon getting Hires' and see that you get no other.

MEATS.

ROAST BEEF.

Lay the meat on a rack in a pan, and dredge all over with salt, pepper and flour. Put it in a very hot oven with two or three tablespoonfuls of drippings of pieces of the beef fat placed in the pan. Put the skin side down at first, that the heat may harden the juices in the lean part. Baste often and dredge twice with salt and flour. When seared all over, turn and bring the skin side up for the final basting and browning. Bake ten minutes to a pound if liked very rare. If there be any danger of burning the fat in the pan, add a little hot water after the flour is browned.

GRAVY.

Remove the meat when done to a heated dish, skim the drippings, add a little boiling water, a little browned flour, and boil up once, then strain it and send to the table in a gravy-boat.

YORKSHIRE PUDDING.

Beat three eggs very light, add salt and one pint of milk, and one cup of flour. Bake in hot gem pans. Baste with the drippings from the beef. Serve as a garnish to roast beef.

POTTED BEEF.

Take a large beef shank and put in cold water. Boil until perfectly tender. Remove bone and cartilage, chop meat fine and replace in the kettle with the liquor which should be one quart. Let it simmer and season with salt, pepper and mace. Press and cut in slices.

BOILED CORN BEEF.

Put the beef in a kettle, and if very salt, cover well with cold water, if only slightly corned, use boiling water, skim while boiling. Boil a piece weighing eight pounds five hours.

MEAT PIE.

Cut two pounds of beef in inch pieces and stew till tender. Remove the meat and add to the water in which it was stewed a little salt, pepper and flour. Line a deep plate with nice paste, put in the meat and turn over it part of the gravy which you have prepared. Add small pieces of butter. Cover with paste; make a gash in the centre, ornament with strips of paste; and bake till the crust is done. Serve with gravy.

STUFFED BEEFSTEAK.

Prepare dressing as for chicken; take flank steak; trim off fat, then spread the dressing on; roll up; tie, and put in a pan with a little water. Bake one hour.

REMNANTS OF ROAST BEEF.

Take pieces left from roast beef. Cut in pieces about the size of dice, put in deep dish, add gravy, season with pepper and salt. Boil potatoes, mash and prepare them as you would for mashed potatoes with the addition of an egg. Put this over the meat, cover and put in the oven and bake about an hour. A short time before it is done, remove the cover and brown.

A GOOD BREAKFAST DISH.

Take small pieces left from roast beef, veal mutton or chicken. Chop fine, season with salt, pepper and onion chopped fine if liked. Cook this up in enough gravy to moisten. Toast slices of bread, dip them in warm water and spread with butter, place the toast on hot platter, spread the chopped mixture on each slice of bread and serve.

IRISH STEW.

Cut two pounds of the neck of mutton into small pieces, put it into a kettle with one onion sliced and a bunch of pot herbs nicely dressed. Simmer gently for one hour, then add two tablespoonfuls of rice, simmer ten minutes, add two potatoes cut into dice, and while they are cooking ten minutes longer, make your dumplings. Put a pint of flour into a bowl, add a teaspoonful of salt and a heaping teaspoonful baking powder, moisten this with a gill of water; the dough must be soft. Form it lightly into balls, drop them on top of the stew, cover the kettle, boil ten minutes, season and serve.

VEAL.

VEAL LOAF.

Three and one half pounds of minced veal (the leg is best for this purpose) three eggs, well beaten, one tablespoonful of pepper, and one salt, one grated nutmeg, four rolled crackers, one tablespoonful of cream, two tablespoonful of butter; mix these together and make into a loaf, roast and baste like other meats.

BREADED VEAL CUTLETS.

Wipe and remove bone and tough membrane from a slice of veal, from the leg, shape for serving, season with salt and pepper, roll in fine cracker crumbs, then egg, and crumbs again. Fry slices of salt pork and brown the cutlets in the fat. Then place in stew pan. Make a brown gravy with one tablespoon butter or pork fat, two of flour, and one and one half cups stock or water. Season with lemon, Worcestershire sauce, horse-radish, or tomato, pour gravy over cutlets, and simmer 45 minutes or till tender.

ROAST VEAL.

Take a loin of veal, make an incision in the flap and fill with dressing, secure it with small skewers and dredge the veal with a little flour, slightly salted. Bake in a moderate oven, and baste often; at first with a little salt and water, and afterward with the drippings in the pan. When done skim the gravy, and thicken with browned flour. Dressing, bread crumbs, chopped thyme and parsley; a little pepper, salt, one egg and a little butter.

MINCED VEAL AND EGGS.

One quart of cold veal chopped rather coarse, one teaspoonful lemon juice, one cup water, two tablespoonfuls of butter, one teaspoonful flour. Heat thoroughly and dish on slices of bread toasted. Put a dropped egg in the centre of each slice and serve very hot.

SWEET-BREADS (Very nice).

Put the sweet-breads in cold water for a few hours; take them out and parboil. Roll in egg and cracker crumbs and fry in butter to a nice brown. On a hot platter have butter, pepper and salt, place the sweet-breads on the platter and serve.

CREAMED SWEET-BREADS.

Place in cold water, remove pipes and membrane, cook in boiling salted water with one tablespoon lemon juice, twenty minutes. Drain, cover with cold water, and change until cold. Cut in dice, and heat in sauce. For one pint, make white sauce with one and one half cups cream and one and one half tablespoonfuls each flour and butter. Season with celery salt, pepper and salt.

MUTTON AND LAMB.

LAMB OR MUTTON CHOP.

Separate from the bone. Broil like beef steak, or to fry dip each chop in beaten egg and cracker crumbs and fry in pork fat. Add salt when half cooked. Have pepper, butter and salt in a hot platter. Place on the chops and serve. Make gravy by turning off the fat and adding water and flour. Let it boil and strain.

MUTTON TURKEY.

Have the bone taken from a good plump leg of mutton and fill the cavity with turkey dressing; sew it up and put the joint in a pot of boiling water, and let boil slowly for half an hour. Take it out with some of the liquor and put in the oven to roast for an hour and a half, basting it frequently. Serve hot with potatoes, turnips, and cranberry or apple sauce.

ESCALLOPED MUTTON.

Cut thin slices of roast meat, free from skin and fat, season with salt and pepper. Place a layer of crumbs in baking dish, then one of meat, then oysters strained and seasoned, then tomato, or brown sauce, then repeat, finishing with thick layer of crumbs. Bake until brown.

PORK.

TO CHOOSE PORK.

The rind should be thin and smooth, the fat thick and white, the lean light of color mixed with little particles of fat.

ROAST PORK.

Wash and dredge well with flour. Place in the pan with a little hot water. Season when half done. Make gravy as for roast beef. Serve apple sauce with roast pork.

PORK CHOPS OR STEAK.

Separate from the bone, dip in beaten egg and cracker and fry as lamb chop.

PORK AND STRING BEANS.

String and cut in small pieces one half peck of beans. Place one half pound of lean salt pork or beef in a kettle of water. Change the water after it has boiled up once. Put in the beans and cook slowly for three or four hours. Let nearly all the water simmer away. Turn into a dish and add milk, butter, pepper and salt, if needed.

BAKED BEANS.

Soak one quart beans over night, pour off the water and cook in fresh water until they crack open; then put into a deep earthen dish, cover with the water, put into the centre of the dish one-half pound of salt pork which should be scored across the rind, add one tablespoonful molasses. Keep nearly covered with water until two thirds done, then allow them to brown. Bake in moderate oven all day.

TO BOIL HAM.

Wash and scrape well. Put into cold water with half a teaspoonful of soda. Boil up once, turn off the water. Add hot water to more than cover the ham. Keep plenty of water in and boil slowly three or four hours. Take out of the kettle and place in a baking pan. Skin and trim well. Spread over the following dressing and bake one half hour.

BOILED HAM DRESSING.

Eight crackers rolled fine and sifted. Beat two eggs well, add two-thirds cup sugar, one teaspoonful mustard, one half teaspoonful cayenne pepper. Wet crackers for swelling before adding eggs and seasoning. Beat all to a thick paste.

BOILED HAM AND EGGS.

Boil two pounds of ham, leaving on the fat till done. Chop fine with four hard boiled eggs. Press and slice cold. If one wishes seasoning add mustard while mixing.

FRIED HAM AND EGGS.

Remove the fat and bone from the ham. Fry the fat to a crisp and place on the platter. Put in the ham, cut in pieces and cook quickly. Place on the platter. Turn off nearly all the fat to fry the eggs in. Make gravy. Fry the eggs and place one on each piece of ham. Garnish with parsley and serve.

HAM AND EGGS.

Chop finely some cold boiled ham, fat and lean together, say a pound to four eggs; put a piece of butter in the pan, then the ham; let it get well warmed through, then beat the eggs light; stir them in briskly.

CREAMED HAM.

One pint minced ham, one pint white sauce, one and one half cups milk, one and one half tablespoons each flour and butter, serve on toast.

FRIED LIVER.

Soak the liver in warm water one half hour. Fry slices of fat salt pork until brown, take out the pork. Dip each piece of liver in flour and fry in the fat. Add salt and pepper while frying. Place the liver on a platter with bits of butter and pour gravy over it.

POULTRY.

ROAST FOWL.

Remove pin feathers, tendons and feet; singe, wash, remove crop, oil bag and entrails; stuff and sew. Skewer and tie in shape. Rub all over with soft butter and dredge with salt, pepper, and flour. Place in the pan in a hot oven, on a rack without water. Baste with one third cup of melted butter in one cup hot water. Dredge with flour after basting, turn and brown on all sides. Add more water if needed, and cover with buttered paper if it browns too fast.

For the *stuffing* moisten one and one half cups grated stale bread crumbs with one third cup melted butter, season highly with salt, pepper and thyme or sweet marjoram, and add a little water.

GRAVY.

Stew the giblets till tender. Save the liquor for the gravy. Thicken with browned flour. Add the chopped giblets and butter. Season to taste.

ROAST GOOSE.

Geese and ducks are better if parboiled before they are roasted. Put them in water to cover and simmer two hours. Make a dressing and roast as you do turkey.

CHICKEN LOAF.

Boil two chickens till quite tender, take out the bones and chop the meat, season to taste with butter, pepper and salt, add enough of the liquor in which it was boiled to make quite moist, put into moulds, turn out when cold and cut in slices.

CHICKEN PIE.

Cut the fowl in pieces. Fry two slices of pork to a crisp in the kettle. Take out the pork and put in the chicken. Cover with hot water and stew till tender. Put the chicken away till cold. Save the broth for gravy. Put three tablespoonfuls of butter into, a small kettle and when hot add three tablespoonfuls of flour. Stir until smooth but not brown, and stir in the broth. Cook ten minutes. Beat one egg with one spoonful of cold water and add the gravy to it. Make a good crust of one quart of flour, one cup of shortening (lard and butter) two teaspoonfuls of baking powder, salt, white of one egg and water. Line the plate. Remove the meat from the bone, fill the plate, pour over some of the gravy, add bits of butter and season to taste. Bake till the crust is done.

FRICASSEE CHICKEN.

Boil till nearly tender, then drain till dry, take half a cup of butter and put in frying-pan, fry till brown, thicken the broth that the chicken was boiled in, serve in a deep dish, turn the gravy over the chicken.

CHICKEN AND CREAM.

Joint one pair of chickens; wash the pieces in cold water, and dry them in a cloth; roll them in fine bread or cracker crumbs. Fry the chicken in butter until nicely browned, and place on a hot dish. Take a pint of rich milk; season with pepper and salt; and thicken with a teaspoonful of flour; pour slowly into the frying pan, stirring briskly until the flour is cooked, then turn over the chicken, and garnish with chopped parsley.

USE THE BEST.

Knickerbocker Roasted Coffees

Select Fruit Extracts.   .   .   .

Finest Quality Ground Spices.

MANUFACTURED BY

THOMSON & TAYLOR SPICE CO.

MICHIGAN AVE. & LAKE STREET,

CHICAGO.

CHICKEN CROQUETTES.

For one dozen croquettes, use one and one half cups chopped chicken, free of bone, skin and gristle. Cook two tablespoons of butter, and two heaping tablespoonfuls of corn-starch one minute, then add one pint hot milk. Season with one spoonfulsalt, one half spoonful celery salt and pepper, one heaping teaspoonful of chopped parsley; two of lemon juice, and a very little onion juice. Spread on platter and cool; then shape into rolls, and roll in crumbs, egg and crumbs again, and fry in hot lard.

VEGETABLES.

—

POTATOES.

Potatoes are much nicer steamed than boiled. If boiled put into salted water and boil till done. Remove from the fire. Turn off the water. Sprinkle on salt and let stand on the back of the stove for five minutes.

CREAMED POTATOES.

Cut one pint cold boiled potatoes into dice, cover with cold milk; when hot add one heaping teaspoonful flour, moistened with a little cold milk; cook ten minutes, then add one tablespoonful butter, one tablespoonful chopped parsley, one half teaspoonful salt and one and one half saltspoonful pepper.

POTATOES A LA ROYAL.

One pint of hot boiled potatoes, a generous half-cupful of cream or milk. two tablespoonfuls of butter, the whites of four eggs and the yolk of one, salt and pepper to taste.   Beat the potato very light and fine.   Add the seasoning, milk and butter, and lastly the whites of the eggs beaten to a stiff froth.   Turn into a buttered escallop dish.   Smooth with a knife, and brush over with the yolk of the egg, which has been well beaten.   Brown quickly and serve.   It will take ten minutes to brown.   The dish in which it is baked should hold a little more than a quart.

ESCALLOPED POTATOES.

Cut up cold boiled potatoes until you have about a quart.   Put in a pan a generous cup of milk, one teaspoonful of flour and one tablespoonful of butter.   Set on the stove and let it thicken, then put a layer of potatoes in a pudding dish, season with salt and pepper, and pour on a little of the gravy.   Continue until all is used.   Cover the top with rolled cracker crumbs and bits of butter.   Bake twenty minutes.

LYONAISE POTATOES.

Six potatoes, parboiled, and when cold, sliced or cut into dice; one half onion, chopped; butter or dripping from frying; chopped parsley, pepper and salt.   Add seasoning and serve dry.

SARATOGA POTATOES.

Shave thin, soak in ice water thirty minutes, fry in boiling lard to light brown, dry and salt.   Serve hot in folded napkin.

POTATO CROQUETTES.

Mix well one pint hot mashed potatoes, with one tablespoon butter, one half teaspoon of salt, one half saltspoon of pepper, a little onion juice, and one teaspoon of chopped parsley, then add yolk of one egg.   Shape in smooth balls, roll in fine bread crumbs, then in beaten egg and crumbs again, place in basket and fry in smoking hot lard.

GRANDMA'S

FOR COUGHS, COLDS.
BRONCHITIS
HOARSENESS
AND ALL DISEASES OF
THROAT AND LUNGS.

Cough

Syrup

PREPARED BY
CHEERYBLE BROTHERS.
CHICAGO, ILLS.

For sale by the **Ladies' Aid Society** of the

ENGLEWOOD

UNIVERSALIST

CHURCH.

Endorsed by the Leading Clergy of Englewood.

SWEET POTATO CROQUETTES.

Boil, peel and mash four good-sized potatoes, add two ounces of butter, a half-teaspoonful of salt and a dash of cayenne; beat until smooth; form into cylinder-shaped croquettes. Dip in egg and then in bread crumbs, and fry in smoking-hot fat.

POTATOES A LA MAITRE DE L'HOTEL.

Use raw potatoes cut in dice, or scooped with potato scoop, cook until tender in salted water, drain and spread the butter over them hot.

Dressing: Mix one tablespoonful of butter with the yolk of one egg; add one teaspoonful lemon juice, and one teaspoonful chopped parsley; one half teaspoonful salt, and one salt-spoonful of pepper.

SMOTHERED POTATOES.

Slice raw potatoes very thin, soak in cold water and squeeze dry. Make three layers in a baking dish, seasoning each layer with salt, pepper, butter and a little minced onion. Pour over each layer a thin white sauce, two tablespoonfuls of flour and one tablespoonful of butter. Bake an hour, or until potatoes are tender.

STEWED ONIONS.

Boil two or three large Spanish onions till very soft; then put them in the oven in a dish with a little butter; bake till brown; taste and turn; and then put them in your dish; dredge flour over the butter left in the dish; add some hot milk. Stir well.

BEETS.

Boil them from one to two hours; take off the skin when done, and put over them pepper, salt and a little butter. Beets are very good baked, but require a much longer time to cook.

PARSNIPS.

Boil parsnips till tender; cut lengthwise and add butter, pepper and salt.

FRIED PARSNIPS.

Cut boiled parsnips lengthwise. Dredge with flour and fry in butter.

GREEN PEAS.

Take one half peck of peas and put in boiling water and cook until soft. Let the water cook nearly away. Remove from the fire and add milk, butter and salt.

ASPARAGUS.

Boil in salted water till tender; toast bread, and dip in the water in which the asparagus was boiled. Lay the asparagus on toast and turn on cream sauce.

SPINACH.

Wash thoroughly, and boil in salted water, or corned beef liquor Press the water out and chop fine. Serve with vinegar and pepper.

TOMATOES.

Turn boiling hot water on and peel, then slice and serve with vinegar, salt and pepper, or sugar.

BROILED TOMATOES.

Cut ripe tomatoes in halves, and sprinkle the cut side with salt, pepper, and cracker or fine bread-crumbs. Place in a double broiler and broil ten minutes over a clear fire, keeping the outside next the fire. Slip carefully on a dish, put a bit of butter on each piece, and place in the oven for ten minutes. Garnish with parsley, and serve.

STUFFED TOMATOES.

Get them as large and firm as possible; cut a round place in the top, scrape out all the soft parts; mix with stale bread crumbs, onions, parsley, butter, pepper and salt; chop very fine, and fill the tomatoes carefully; bake in a moderately hot oven; put a little butter in the pan, and see that they do not burn or become dry.

CEYLON

PURE

SPICES

Choicest Importations.

❋ ❋ ❋

GROUND AND PACKED BY

Franklin MacVeagh & Co.

CHICAGO.

STEWED CORN.

Scald the corn just enough to harden; slice off the ear so as to divide the kernel three or four times; scrape the chits (the sweetest part) from the cob, add sweet milk, a little water, a little butter and salt—simmer ten minutes. Beat one egg and add, stirring in evenly just before taking off the fire. A very little sugar improves it for the taste of most people.

CREAMED CORN.

To one or more cans of corn, add a cup of milk, salt and pepper to taste, and a piece of butter the size of an egg. When nearly ready to serve make a teaspoonful of flour smooth with a little cream, and stir in very gradually; when it is thoroughly heated, it is ready to serve.

CORN FRITTERS.

One pint grated corn. one half cup milk, one half cup flour, one small teaspoonful baking powder, one tablespoonful melted butter, two eggs, one teaspoonful salt, a little pepper, fry in hot lard.

MACARONI OR SPAGHETTI WITH CHEESE.

One quarter pound or twelve sticks of macaroni or spaghetti broken into one inch lengths, and cooked in three pints boiling salted water twenty minutes. Turn into a colander and pour over it cold water, drain. Make a sauce of one tablespoonful flour and one tablespoonful of butter, and one and one half cups of hot milk, salt. Put a layer of grated cheese in bottom of bake dish, then a layer of macaroni and sauce, cover the top with fine bread crumbs with bits of butter dotted over, and a little grated cheese. Bake, until brown.

FRIED SWEET POTATOES.

For a nice breakfast dish, parboil sweet potatoes on the day before. When cold cut them in lengthwise slices, and fry to a nice brown in butter or beef drippings. Sprinkle with salt and pepper.

TURNIPS A LA CREME.

Take small new turnips, peel and boil them in salted water; drain them thoroughly. Melt one ounce of butter in a saucepan, add to it a dessert-spoonful of flour, pepper, salt, and a small quantity of milk or cream; put in the turnips; simmer gently a few minutes, and serve.

BOILED ONIONS.

Remove the outer skins from a sufficient number of small yellow onions, parboil them with water, which should be put on cold, and when tender, but not broken, add to them a cup of cold milk, some salt, pepper, and a piece of butter, then let them boil up gently in this mixture, and serve.

CAULIFLOWER.

Soak the cauliflower in very salt cold water for two or three hours. Have four quarts of boiling water in which has been added a small table-spoonful of salt, and a saltspoonful of soda. Take the cauliflower out of the cold water, break into sections. Tie it in a twine bag while boiling, put it into the kettle of boiling water, and let it cook rapidly for an hour, drain, and serve with butter, salt and pepper, or cream sauce.

ESCALLOPED ONIONS, CAULIFLOWER OR ASPARAGUS.

Boil either vegetable until tender, then put in baking dish, and pour over sauce made of one tablespoonful butter rubbed into one and one half tablespoonfuls of flour, pour over it one pint hot milk and cook until like custard. Bake half an hour. Cut cauliflower or asparagus into small pieces before pouring over the sauce.

EGGS.

ESCALLOPED EGGS.

Make a minced meat of chopped ham, fine bread crumbs, pepper, salt, and some melted butter. Moisten with milk to a soft paste, and half fill small patty pans with the mixture. Break an egg carefully upon the top of each. Dust with pepper and salt, and sprinkle some finely powdered cracker over all. Set in the oven and bake about eight minutes. Eat hot, they are very nice.

EGGS ON TOAST.

Put one half pint of milk in spider. Toast six slices of bread. Dip the crusts in the hot milk. Place each slice on a platter and butter well. Beat five eggs, add to the hot milk and stir till it thickens. Season with salt and pepper, add a large piece of butter and serve on the toast.

SCRAMBLED EGGS.

Nine eggs, not beaten, butter, pepper and salt. Have butter in the spider, and when the butter is hot, put in the eggs and begin at once to stir them, scraping the bottom of the pan from the sides toward the centre, until you have a soft, moist mass just firm enough not to run over the bottom of the heated dish on which you turn it out.

EGG VERMICELLI.

Cook six eggs twenty minutes, separate whites and yolks. Chop whites, and add one and one half cups white sauce, season, cover a platter with small squares of toast, cover with the white sauce, and strain the yolks over it, through fruit-press. Garnish with parsley.

EGG OMELET.

Separate the whites from the yolks of four eggs, beat the whites stiff, then beat the yolks stiff, add salt-spoonful of salt, and one half salt-spoonful of pepper, four tablespoonfuls of milk; mix them with spoon, pour this mixture over the whites and mix them, by using knife, butter your pan and have not too hot a fire.

WELSH RAREBIT.

Break a quarter of a pound of cheese in small pieces, or if hard, grate it, and put in double boiler with quarter of a cup of rich milk or cream. Mix one teaspoon of mustard, half a spoon of salt and a little pepper. Add one egg and beat well and when the cheese is melted stir this in with a teaspoon of butter. Cook until it thickens and pour over slices of hot toast. Serve immediately.

SALADS.

—

POTATO SALAD.

Cut cold boiled potatoes in dice or thin slices; make about three layers of potatoes in salad dish, seasoning each layer with a little minced parsley onion and beet dice and boiled dressing.

BOILED DRESSING.

One tablespoon flour, one teaspoon each of mustard and salt, two table-spoons of sugar, one fourth salt-spoon red pepper, one half cup vinegar, three fourths cup water, one tablespoon butter and yolks of three eggs. Mix the dry ingredients and carefully add vinegar and water and heat boiling hot. Have yolks of eggs well beaten and slowly pour on the boiling hot mixture, beating all the time; add the butter in small pieces.

FRENCH DRESSING.

One saltspoon salt, one half saltspoon pepper, three tablespoons oil, one tablespoon vinegar, a little onion juice. Mix in the order given and pour over the salad.

CHICKEN SALAD.

Use equal quantities of chicken and celery cut fine, season with salt and pepper and mix with

MAYONAISE DRESSING.

Have dish, oil and eggs, cold. For one large bottle of oil, use four or five yolks of eggs. Stir or beat with something that will mix rapidly, a wooden paddle is preferred. Be careful not to pour oil any faster than eggs take it up. When thick enough to take up on the beater like a ball, use a little vinegar or lemon juice to thin it. When nearly done season with one teaspoon each of mustard and salt, and one half saltspoon of Cayenne pepper to one pint of oil. Use enough acid to taste well and make the right consistency.

TARTARE SAUCE.

To Mayonaise dressing add capers, chopped cucumbers, pickles, olives, and parsley, one or all.

SALAD DRESSING WITH BUTTER OR OIL.

Mix well two tablespoons sugar, one level one of mustard and a teaspoonful of salt. Add one and one half tablespoons of Olive oil or two and one half tablespoons melted butter. Then add three well beaten eggs gradually, then three fourths cup of vinegar and one cup of milk. Place in farina kettle over boiling water and stir until thick. This keeps nicely in a cool place and is equally good for a nice salad or for lettuce and cold slaw.

OYSTER SALAD.

Wash and parboil one pint of large oysters. Prepare an equal amount of celery as for chicken salad, mix together and add

CREAM DRESSING.

Beat four whole eggs or eight yolks, add one teaspoon corn starch wet with a little cold water, and one half cup vinegar. Cook in double boiler until thickened. Then add one large tablespoon of butter, one teaspoon of mustard, one half teaspoon salt, one eighth teaspoon pepper; when cold, dilute with thick cream plain or whipped.

STRING BEAN SALAD (Very nice.)

Cook one can string beans as for the table, but pour off the liquor when done. Cut two good sized beets, boiled tender, into half inch dice. Cut the whites of four hard boiled eggs into neat pieces. Mix carefully without breaking, the beets, whites of eggs and string beans (which should be cut not more than one and a half inches long), add the "Salad Dressing with Butter or Oil" and when arranged in dish rub through a sieve the yolks of two of the eggs on the salad. A few of the beet dice may be reserved to add last in garnishing.

LOBSTER SALAD.

One head of lettuce is sufficient for a can of lobster. Break the meat carefully, reserving the coral for garnishing. Cut up fine one half of the lettuce and mix with lobster, adding the dressing at the same time. Arrange on the remaining lettuce and garnish.

The Tartare sauce is very nice to use with the fresh lobster when it can be obtained.

CAULIFLOWER SALAD (Very nice).

Boil the finest head of cauliflower until tender. Cut into individual pieces, very carefully, dipping each in melted butter, containing a little onion juice, if liked. Let the pieces drain until cold. Then mix with hard boiled eggs and dressing.

SALMON AND SHRIMP SALADS.

These can be prepared like lobster salad.

CABBAGE SALAD.

For two quarts chopped cabbage, one half pint cider vinegar, one teaspoon salt, one teaspoon mustard, one half teaspoonful black pepper, one tablespoon sugar, one tablespoon butter. When it comes to a boil, stir in two well beaten eggs until thickened. Pour over cabbage. Garnish with slices of hard boiled eggs.

LOBSTER SALAD.

Chop a good sized lobster very fine, reserving the small claws, and coral for garnishing, into this lobster chop a head of lettuce, saving a few leaves to help garnish. Mix lobster with salad dressing on a platter, placing coral, leaves and claws around the edge.

SALMON SALAD.

One can of salmon, or the same quantity of any cold fish, preferably boiled or baked, from which the skin and bones have been removed. Chop, when cold, three large boiled potatoes, and mix them with the fish. Rub smooth the yolk of three hard-boiled eggs, season to taste with mustard, pepper and salt, add two tablespoonfuls of cream and one gill of vinegar. Pour this dressing over the fish and potatoes. This may either be served by itself, or a nest can be made of leaves of lettuce and the fish and potatoes placed in it, or the lettuce leaves can be placed around the edge of the dish and served with each portion.

BREAD, Etc.

BREAD.

Put one tablespoon of sugar, one tablespoon of lard and one teaspoon of salt, in a large bowl. Scald one cup of milk and pour over them. When dissolved add one and one half cups water; dissolve one half cake yeast in one half cup of water and add when the mixture is lukewarm. Add sifted flour until stiff enough to mold. Mold until smooth, cover well and set to rise; cut it down and mold from fifteen minutes to half an hour; shape into loaves, put in pans, rise and bake.

GRAHAM BREAD.

One cup milk, two cups water, one tablespoon lard, three tablespoons of sugar, one teaspoon salt, one half cake yeast. Treated the same as white bread without molding.

ROLLS.

One cup milk, one fourth cup butter, one half teaspoon salt, one table- spoon sugar one fourth cake yeast dissolved in one fourth cup water, white of one egg. Treat like white bread. When risen light cut down with a knife, roll on molding board one half inch thick, cut with a biscuit cutter. Butter one half and fold the other half over; let rise and bake.

The Quaker's Cooking Recipe.

FOR BREAKFAST.

1st.—Be sure that thee gets **QUAKER OATS**. They are sold only in two-pound packages.

2d.—After lighting thy fire, put two tin pans full of water in a hot place forthwith, and mix a handful of dry **QUAKER OATS**, with a pinch of salt in another tin pan.

3d.—When both pans of water be boiling—not before—place the pan of dry **QUAKER OATS** in one of them. Pour the contents of the other pan on the **QUAKER OATS** to more than cover them, place a tin cover over both pans and boil thirty minutes or more.

NOTE.

The old gentleman was born in Philadelphia and is never in a hurry. Shorten his time for cooking it necessary.   ED.

TRADE MARK

G. W. DUNBAR'S SONS,

NEW ORLEANS, LA.,

PACKERS OF

FRESH SHRIMP, for Salads and Mayonaise.

GREEN TURTLE, for Soup.

FRESH OKRA, for Soup.

ARTICHOKES, for Entrees.

PRESERVED FIGS, for the Tea Table.

CREOLE PEPPER SAUCE.

SUGAR CANE SYRUP, for Table Use.

FINGER ROLLS.

Having cut down the dough, take small pieces and roll with the hand into finger shapes not over two inches long and quite small around. Place on pan leaving space enough for rising without touching; rise and bake.

SOUP STICKS.

Roll the dough out quite thin and cut in narrow strips, rise and bake.

SWEDISH ROLLS.

Roll out thin; brush over with butter, sprinkle on granulated sugar, a little grated lemon peel, a little cinnamon, dried currants; then roll slowly; cut into inch slices and bake.

POP OVERS.

One cup milk, one cup of flour, a pinch of salt, two eggs. Sift flour and salt together. Add the milk slowly to make a smooth batter. Beat the eggs very light and mix carefully. Cook in hot buttered gem pans or cups half an hour.

BROWN BREAD.

Sift together one cup of corn meal and one of flour with a teaspoon of salt; add two thirds of a cup of molasses and water to make a medium batter; add last two thirds of a teaspoon of soda dissolved in water. Place in two well greased pint cans or one large one and cover tight. Steam two hours and bake half hour or more if in one can.

DROP BISCUIT.

Sift one pint of flour with a heaping teaspoon of baking powder and and a pinch of salt. Rub in one half tablespoon each of lard and butter. Make a dough with milk until nearly as stiff as for regular biscuits and drop from spoon into greased muffin pans. Bake in a hot oven about fifteen minutes.

MUFFINS.

Mix a tablespoon of butter and two tablespoons of sugar, add a cup of milk and two large cups of flour sifted with a heaping teaspoon of baking powder. Then add a small cup of water and last two beaten eggs. Bake about twenty-five minutes in muffin pans.

FRITTERS.

To one and a half cups of milk add beaten yolks of two eggs and one large teaspoon baking powder sifted with flour to make a stiff batter. Beat the whites stiff with a pinch of salt and mix in lightly. Fry by spoonfuls in hot lard. Serve promptly.

APPLE FRITTERS.

Cut apple in slices, dip in the batter and fry in boiling fat. Sprinkle well with sugar.

GRAHAM GEMS.

Beat an egg with two tablespoons of sugar, add one tablespoon soft butter, a little salt, one and one half cups milk, two cups graham flour and one of white sifted with three tablespoons baking powder. Bake in a hot oven.

DUMPLINGS.

Sift two cups of flour with one large teaspoon baking powder, one teaspoon sugar, one teaspoon salt, wet with milk until just soft enough to handle. Roll one half inch thick, cut out and cook ten minutes in boiling liquid closely covered, or steam twenty minutes in steamer.

BAKING POWDER BISCUIT.

Two teaspoons baking powder sifted into one pint of flour, one large spoonful of butter or lard and salt. Rub the shortening into the flour until smooth. Mix with milk or water until stiff enough to handle. Roll one half inch thick and cut.

STRAWBERRY SHORT CAKE.

Mix a little softer than baking powder biscuits using more butter. Divide the mixture into two parts, roll out half an inch thick, place in pan with melted butter between the layers. Bake in a hot oven; divide and fill with mashed berries sweetened with powdered sugar.

STRAWBERRY SHORT CAKE.

One pint of flour, one and a half teaspoonfuls of baking powder and salt sifted with it. One fourth cup of butter, one egg, one scant cup of milk. Bake in a hot oven. Remove from the pan, cut in half with a warm knife. Take out some of the soft bread and fill with mashed berries sweetened with powdered sugar. Put a layer of berries on top and serve with sauce.

SAUCE.

Stir one tablespoonful of corn starch in one pint of boiling water. Add sugar and salt. Pour into tureen, over two spoonfuls of mashed berries and a small piece of butter.

ORANGE SHORT CAKE.

Take a dozen good small, juicy oranges, peel and put in a cold place. Make a shortcake of a pint of prepared flour, a tablespoon of lard and the same of butter rubbed well together and made into a dough with a cup of sour milk. Roll out about an inch thick into a sheet, put into a well buttered pan and bake in a quick oven a light brown. Take out of the pan, and with a sharp knife divide in two as a biscuit. Spread the oranges, thinly sliced, between the cake, sprinkling well with sugar, put the rest on top, and cover with sugar just before sending to the table. Eat with sauce made from the juice of three oranges and two lemons boiled in a pint of water and seasoned with sugar and nutmeg.

BROWN BREAD.

One cup molasses, one cup of sour milk, two cups sweet milk, three cups graham flour, one and one half cups corn meal, one half teaspoon soda. Take graham flour add corn meal, then add sweet milk, then sour milk with soda dissolved in it, then molasses, pinch of salt; steam three hours and bake twenty minutes.

GRIDDLE CAKES.

One pint of flour, salt, one teaspoonful soda, one scant pint of sour milk, two eggs well beaten.

CALIFORNIA MUSH.

Take one part California Breakfast Food and stir into two parts boiling water which has already been salted. Cook ten minutes, serve with cream and sugar.

FRIED BREAKFAST FOOD.

To two teacupfuls of mush made from California Breakfast Food add one egg, when cold slice it and roll in flour. Fry to a nice brown, serve hot.

CALIFORNIA PUDDING.

Take two teacupfuls of the California Breakfast Food cooked as for mush, one pint of milk, two eggs, a little nutmeg, a few raisins, sweeten to taste and bake twenty minutes. Serve with sauce.

WE can cheerfully recommend PET-TIJOHN'S CALIFORNIA BREAKFAST FOOD as a first-class article for making Mush, Griddle Cakes, Gems and Pudding.

Yours truly,

C. WOLF, Chief Cook,
Grand Pacific Hotel.

W. H. PHILLIPS, Cook,
Auditorium Hotel.

J. B. SMITH, Cook, Thomson Restaurant.

J. BAKER, Cook, - Tremont House.

J. HOFF, Cook, - Sherman House.

Pettijohn's California Breakfast Food

Is California White Wheat,

Pearled, Steamed and Rolled through Heated Rollers, it is Packed and Sealed at once so that it Retains all its Freshness. It is a very desirable change from Oats for breakfast. Makes splendid Gems, Griddle Cakes and Pudding. It contains the same properties as Graham, so that we all know that it is very wholesome. Try a package and you will be convinced that it is just what you have been wanting. Costs no more than Oats and is much better. (See recipes in this Cook Book and on packages.)

FOR SALE BY ALL GROCERS.

RAMER & LAW, General Agents, 47 W. Washington Street, Chicago.

PASTRY.

ROUGH PUFF PASTE.

Have both materials and utensils cold. Take one pound of pastry flour and three quarters of a pound of butter and chop together. Make a hole in the centre of this in which place the yolks of two eggs, a pinch of salt and two teaspoons of lemon juice, also two tablespoons of water. Break the egg with a knife and lightly mix it all with the fingers, using more water if necessary to form a stiff paste. Handle lightly and keep hands and board well floured. Pound and roll the paste into an oblong sheet half an inch thick, fold the outer edges in to meet and the ends to nearly meet; then double, roll and fold three or more times. Chill on ice.

PLAIN PASTE.

Use one and one half rounded cups of unsifted pastry flour and half a cup of lard, half a teaspoon of salt and cold water enough to made a stiff paste. Mix dry together lightly with tips of the fingers and mix in water carefully with a knife in warm weather or fingers in cold.

ANOTHER PLAIN PASTE.

To one and one half cups of flour take one third of a cup each of lard and butter; rub in all the lard and half of the butter and roll the remainder of the butter into the upper crust.

Crystal Rice

THE BEST OF ALL

CEREAL FOOD PRODUCTS.

PURE . . . .

HEALTHFUL

CONVENIENT

MANUFACTURED BY

Crystal Rice Milling Company,

MARION, INDIANA.

JAMES B. ALBACH, Agent,

26 RIVER ST., CHICAGO.

CINCINNATI, O., Nov. 12th, 1896.

THE CRYSTAL MILLING Co., Marion, Ind.

DEAR SIRS:—Please ship us at once two barrels of Crystal Rice. We find it the most popular, with our guests, of any of the new cereal preparations ever placed on our bill of fare, as well as the most economical for use; we have tried it in all kinds of plain cooking and pastry with equally satisfactory results. Wishing you the success your Crystal Rice so well merits, we remain,

Yours truly, THE PALACE HOTEL CO.

LEMON PIE.

Use three-fourths of a cup of sugar, two teaspoons of flour, mix well and add three beaten yolks and one beaten white. Then add juice and grated rind of one lemon with half a cup of cold water. Bake in an open crust of pastry until it shakes like jelly. Let it cool, before adding meringue made by beating the two remaining whites till dry and gradually beating in two tablespoons of powdered sugar. Brown in a hot oven.

FRUIT PIES.

Pile fruit high in the center leaving a space around the sides nearly bare. When the cover is on press the paste gently into this grove, then make several deep holes in the groove. The juice will run in the groove instead of wasting through the edges. Rhubarb should not be peeled, but washed, sliced fine, scalded half an hour, drained and well dredged with flour.

NEW ENGLAND MINCE PIES.

Stew one package of Dougherty's New England Condensed Mince Meat with a quart of water for twenty minutes. Sugar, fruit syrup, vinegar or any preserves may be added to suit the taste, in this case use less water.

MINCE MEAT.

Two and one half pounds meat.
Five pounds of apples.
Two pounds sugar.
Half pound butter.
One pint molasses.
Four teaspoons cinnamon.
Three teaspoons cloves.
Five teaspoons nutmeg.
One quart cider.
Two pounds raisins.

CAKE.

POUND CAKE.

Beat half a pound of butter to a cream, add three fourths of a pound of sugar gradually, beating until all is light. Measure half a pint of eggs, whites and yolks separate. Beat the yolks well and add to sugar and butter, then the stiff whites. Beat again and add three-fourths of a pound of flour. In using fruit, sprinkle with flour, warm and add last. Bake in moderate oven.

SPONGE CAKE.

Beat yolks of four eggs until light colored and thick, gradually beat in one cup of powdered sugar, add juice and grated rind of a lemon and beat again. Beat the whites stiff and dry and cut in lightly, then sift in one cup of flour and cut and fold carefully. Bake in very moderate oven about forty-five minutes.

WHITE CAKE.

Cream one-third of a cup of butter, beat in two cups of sugar, add a spoon of vanilla and stir in two and one half cups of flour sifted with a teaspoon of baking powder. Mix in lightly the stiff whites of eight eggs. Bake in a moderate oven until done. Test with a broom splint.

LAYER CAKE.

Cream half a cup of butter, add two cups of sugar, and milk enough from a cupful to mix easily. Flavor with vanilla, then sift in three cups of pastry flour with three spoons of baking powder, alternately with the rest of the milk. Add last the stiff whites of four eggs. Bake in four layers in rather hot oven.

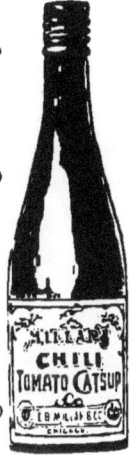

CARAMEL FILLING.

Use two cups of sugar, two thirds of a cup of milk and a tablespoon of butter. Boil seven minutes, cool and spread. A square of melted chocolate may be added.

FIG FILLING.

Boil until thick one cup of water, one cup of sugar and half a pound of chopped figs.

BANANA FILLING.

Chop fine or mash nine large ripe bananas, sweeten with powdered sugar and spread between layers. This must be eaten while fresh.

LEMON FILLING.

Beat the whites of two eggs stiff, add one large cup of powdered sugar and the grated rind and juice of two lemons. Thicken in a double boiler.

PLAIN FROSTING.

To the white of one egg add one tablespoon of water and a few drops of vanilla extract, or lemon juice. Then stir in powdered sugar until thick enough to spread. This is sufficent for a large layer cake.

CHOCOLATE FROSTING.

Use above recipe and add one square of melted chocolate.

NUT FILLING.

Double the rule for plain frosting and add half a pound of English walnuts chopped fine. Use between the layers and on top.

ONE WOMAN'S IDEA. ❋ ❋ ❋

Inventors have long sought a suitable method of canning fruit and other foods *without cooking or the use of chemicals.* Hundreds of dollars and years of patient labor have been expended, but it has been reserved for a woman—Miss Amanda T. Jones, of Chicago—to be the inventor of this hitherto undiscovered process. The practicability of the process being established, a company has been incorporated with $1,000,000 capitalization under the name of

THE WOMAN'S CANNING & PRESERVING CO.

Manufacturing was begun in January of this year. The first product—lunch tongues—(for the process is applicable to cooked foods as well), has produced the verdict from wholesale dealers, that with such improvements the whole canning industry will be revolutionized. Three factories, besides the one now in operation, will be established before autumn.

The new process consists of *placing the cans in a hollow chest from which the air has been expelled by hot steam and that in turn condensed by spraying cold water without.* This produces a *vacuum* and the cans are then sealed by delicate machinery. As every particle of gas is thus expelled from the canned goods, *decomposition is impossible. The process further is so simple that its cost is relatively less than the ordinary methods.*

The following are officers and prominent stockholders:

HELEN M. HOOD, Secretary Ill. W. C. T. U.
MARY ALLEN WEST, Editor "Union Signal.
MRS. J. B. HOBBS, Chicago, Ill.
MRS. SENATOR DOLPH, Washington, D. C.
MISS PHOEBE COUZINS, Ex-Secretary Board Lady Managers World's Fair.
MME. DEMOREST, Philadelphia, Pa.

Stock is now being sold at

· · · · $25.00 PER SHARE · · · ·

but is bound to increase in value. *It is absolutely non-assessable.* Send for circulars and information. Mention cook book in writing us.

Call on or address,

WOMAN'S CANNING & PRESERVING CO.

42 Portland Block, Chicago. **G. L. Wilson, Agt.**

CREAM FILLINC.

Place in double boiler a pint of milk. Beat together the yolks of four eggs, two tablespoons of flour and four of sugar. When milk is scalded add the beaten mixture and a pinch of salt. Stir until smooth, then cook fifteen minutes, stirring frequently. When cool flavor with vanilla and spread on two layers.

PINE-APPLE FILLINC.

Take the juice from one can of grated pine apple, which will be about a cupful; thicken on the stove with one tablespoon of corn starch, then add one beaten yolk to the hot mixture and one third of a cup of sugar. Remove from the stove and stir in half of the remaining pulp.

HOT TEA CAKE.

Beat two eggs well and add three-fourths of a cup of sugar. Then add alternately one cup of milk and two of flour sifted with three teaspoons of baking powder. Beat well, add two tablespoons of melted butter and bake in a shallow pan in a rather hot oven for half an hour.

CINCERBREAD.

Mix one cupful each of sour cream and molasses, add two small spoons of ginger and a pinch of salt. Dissolve two level teaspoons of soda in a tablespoon of water and stir into the mixture. Add a well beaten egg and two cups of flour. Beat well and bake twenty minutes in a hot oven.

DOUCHNUTS.

Beat one egg very well; add one cup of sugar, half a teaspoon of salt and one cup of sour milk. Then sift in nearly a quart of flour with a small spoon each of cinnamon and cloves. Add three tablespoons of melted butter and a teaspoon of soda dissolved in water. Roll half an inch thick. Fry in hot lard.

NUT COOKIES.

Beat two eggs light, add one cup of sugar, and a cup of flour sifted with a small spoon of baking powder and a pinch of salt. Mix in one cup of finely chopped walnuts or hickory nuts. Drop by teaspoonful an inch apart in large pan and bake in a moderate oven.

ALMOND COOKIES.

Cream half a pound of butter, add same amount of powdered sugar, two well beaten eggs, half a pound of grated almonds and the same amount of flour. Spread the cookies with beaten egg and it is well to reserve part of the sugar and nuts to sprinkle on top.

BOILED ICING.

Boil one cup of granulated sugar and one third of a cup of water until it hairs. Do not stir. Have the white of an egg beaten stiff and when the sugar is ready beat it into the egg, pouring in a small stream. Beat until ready for the cake, flavor with a teaspoon of lemon juice and spread. If it thickens too quickly add hot water, a teaspoonful at a time.

PRESERVES AND PICKLES.

JAM.

Strawberries, blackberries or raspberries make good jam and if put up air tight three fourths sugar is sufficient, but put in glasses like jelly it is it is best to make it pound for pound.   It should be cooked three quarters of an hour and must be carefully watched to prevent burning.   The best way to cover jam and jelly is with melted parafine, which excludes all air.

PINE-APPLE.

The best way to retain the natural flavor is to put equal quantities of granulated sugar and grated pine-apple in small jars and cover tightly.   It is delicious for ices, creams or puddings.

SPICED CURRANTS.

For five pounds of currants use four of sugar, a pint of vinegar and two tablespoons each of cinnamon and cloves.   Simmer two hours and place in jars.   Gooseberries or grapes may be done the same.

PIE PLANT :PRESERVE.

Use equal amount of pie plant cut fine and sugar.   Place pie plant in the kettle with a little water and cook until the juices come, add the sugar and simmer an hour.

CHILI SAUCE.

Put in kettle nine large tomatoes, two cups of vinegar, one tablespoon of salt and four of sugar.   Add a large onion chopped with three green peppers, then a teaspoon of each of the spices.   Boil one hour, fill bottles and seal.

☀ TENNESSEE BAKE PAN. ☀

No Burning, No Scorching,

Self=Basting,
No Parboiling,

Bakes
Meats, Fowl, Fish, Game,
Puddings, Cakes
and Bread.

There are many other bake pans which claim to do all the Tennessee Bake Pan does, but wherever this bake pan is introduced it immediately crowds out all others and at once establishes itself with the people for the following reasons:

1. Because it retains all the juices and flavor of the meat.
2. Because it cooks quicker and more evenly.
3. Because almost any sort of tough beef and fowls can be cooked done and tender in it.
4. Because nothing can be burned or scorched while cooking in it.
5. Because two or more different articles can be cooked in the same pan at one time, and each retain its distinct taste and flavor.
6. Because it saves time, trouble, worry, and even fuel, and makes anything cooked in it more pleasant to the taste and more nutritious.

We ask you only to give our invention an examination and fair trial and you will be convinced of its merits. It does more than we claim for it.

From wife of Gov. W. J. Northen, of Ga.: The (Tennessee) Bake Pan reached me in safety. Accept my thanks. It gives me pleasure to testify to its merits. I am much pleased with it. Respectfully,
MRS. W. J. NORTHEN,
Atlanta, Ga.

From the wife of ex-Gov. Robert L. Taylor, of Tenn.: I take pleasure in saying that the Tennessee Bake Pan is all that you claim for it, and will recommend it to all who wish a good pan. Respectfully,
MRS. ROBERT L. TAYLOR,
Chattanooga, Tenn.

Buy the Tennessee Bake Pan. Try it THOROUGHLY, FOLLOWING DIRECTIONS CLOSELY. Then if it fails, notify us, and we WILL REFUND YOUR MONEY. Thus far we have never had a pan returned, nor had to refund the money, because they are *the best on earth.*

Send for descriptive circular and price list. Agents wanted.

Q. A. TIPTON, Jr., Loudon, Tenn.

PICALLILI.

Chop fine one peck of green tomatoes, and two small onions, add one cup of coarse salt and let this stand over night. In the morning drain, and cook one hour then drain dry. Prepare half a gallon of vinegar, half a pound of mustard seed, two chopped red peppers, two pounds of brown sugar, one tablespoon of cinnamon and half a one each of ground cloves, allspice, ginger and whole cloves; add a horse radish root cut in pieces. Let this all boil ten minutes, pour it over the pickle, stir well and place in jars.

CRANBERRY JELLY.

Take a quart each of berries and water and boil until very soft; spread a cheese cloth over colander and strain to get all the juice. Return to the kettle and to each pint of juice add one cup of sugar. Boil until a drop held in the air a few moments will congeal, then pour into moulds.

CHOW CHOW.

Cut up one peck of tomatoes, six small peppers and four onions. Add one cup of salt and soak all night. Drain in the morning add one table-spoon each of cloves, allspice and cinnamon, two pounds of sugar and half a cup of grated horse radish. Cover with vinegar and boil until tender.

IT is an old saw that "The Lord furnishes the *food* and the Devil the *cooks*." But that was *before* this book was published and if its recipes are closely followed and *only* the *best material* used, the saying will pass into "*innocuous desuetude*," and this leads us to say that the *place* to *purchase* the *best groceries* is that place where *quality* is the *first consideration* in the selection of stock. Such a place is John D. Jones', 6159 Wentworth Avenue. Stock complete, choice and fresh, honest goods, honest prices, honest weights. Give him a trial order.

PUDDINGS AND DESSERTS.

FIG PUDDING.

One cup suet, one cup of bread crumbs, one cup of sugar, one half pound figs, three eggs, one cup of milk, one teaspoonful vanilla, nutmeg, two teaspoons baking powder. Steam three hours.

SAUCE.

One cup sugar, one tablespoon of butter, one teaspoonful flour, one cup water, one teaspoon lemon extract. Boil until thick.

COTTAGE PUDDING.

One egg, one cup of sugar, two spoonfuls melted butter, one pint of flour, two teaspoonfuls of baking powder. Bake quickly and eat with sauce. Serve with chocolate sauce.

PUDDING SAUCE FOR COTTAGE PUDDING.

One cup sugar, one-third cup butter, one tablespoon cornstarch, beat all together then pour over it two cups boiling water. After taking from the stove add one egg well beaten, stir quickly and add one half lemon sliced.

CHOCOLATE PUDDING.

One half cup of sugar, one egg, one cup of milk, two squares of melted chocolate, two teaspoonfuls of baking powder sifted with two cups of flour. Steam two hours. Serve with sauce.

EVERY WOMAN SHOULD HAVE IT

"WOMANKIND"

A WEEKLY NEWSPAPER FOR AND ABOUT WOMEN.

WOMANKIND is a consolidation of WOMAN AND HOME, a monthly magazine of high character, for many years published at Philadelphia and New York City, and the WOMAN'S NEWS, a weekly newspaper devoted to general and important news concerning women all over the world.

The policy of the new publication, WOMANKIND, will be, so far as possible, to combine the best features of both papers into one, thus making one of the best woman's papers ever published.

PRICE ONLY $1.00 PER YEAR.

Send for sample copy and see our magnificent premium offers.

Address,

THE HOSTERMAN PUBLISHING CO..

SPRINGFIELD, OHIO.

INDIAN PUDDING.

To one half pint hot water add two-thirds cup Indian meal, stir until it thickens. Add large piece butter, salt, one half cup brown sugar. When cool add one quart milk, two well beaten eggs. Place in the oven and add one cup of cold milk. Bake slowly, when partly done add one half cup raisins. As it dries away add more milk. Bake five or six hours.

APPLE PUDDING.

One egg, one cup sugar, piece of butter size of an egg, two-thirds cup of milk, one teaspoon cinnamon, one teaspoon cream of tarter, $\frac{1}{2}$ teaspoon soda, a little salt, one large cup of sliced apples, flour to make a batter. Bake as a cake. Serve hot, with butter or sauce.

PEACH PUDDING.

Remove the skin and stone of a quart of peaches and cover with one cupful of sugar. One pint and a half of milk heated, two table-spoonfuls of corn starch, two tablespoonfuls of sugar, yolks of three eggs, stir until it thickens. Use the three whites for frosting.

TAPIOCA PUDDING.

One cup pearl tapioca, one quart boiling water, let stand one hour, add two teacups sugar, a little lemon or vanilla, put in six apples quartered or peaches if preferred. Bake one hour.

STRAWBERRY FOAM.

One box of strawberries pressed through a sieve, add two-thirds cup of sugar and beaten whites of three eggs. Beat well and serve with boiled custard.

LEMON JELLY NO. I.

Pour two cups of boiling water on one sheet of isinglass; let it dissolve. Add the juices of two lemons to one cup of sugar, then stir this into the water and strain.

OUR BABY.

HOW TO KEEP THE LITTLE ONES WELL.

What will a mother give to save the life of her child?
All that she has.

And yet it is such a simple thing to keep the baby well, when you know how.

If the nursing mother is weak and out of health, the babe will vomit its food and soon be seriously ill. Or if improper food is used, dangerous illness will result.

Thousands of intelligent mothers and careful physicians have found Lactated Food the best one they could use. It is pure, nourishing and strength-giving.

"I have thoroughly tried the other infant foods on the market, and speak advisedly when I say there is no other food that so thoroughly agrees and nourishes as Lactated Food. I feel that it saved the life of my own fourteen months old boy. N. P. TYLER, M.D., New Rochelle, N.Y., Oct. 14, 1890.

Lactated Food is sold by druggists, or mailed on receipt of price, 25 cents, 50 cents, $1.00. Interesting book of "Prize Babies" and handsome birthday card free to any mother sending baby's name and age.

In writing us, mention Cook Book.

WELLS, RICHARDSON & CO., Burlington, Vt.

DO YOU OWN TOKOLOGY?

A BOOK FOR EVERY WOMAN.

Mrs. M. S. Ramsey writes: Three years since I procured TOKOLOGY, a complete Ladies' Guide in health and disease. I followed its teaching in two instances with happiest results. I cannot say enough in its praise I ask every woman: Have you read Tokology—if not, then get it at once—its value cannot be estimated in money.

N. R. McC. writes: "Dear Dr. Stockham: I shall not attempt to express how thankful I am that you wrote Tokology. I cannot tell you how much it has done for me. Our son came almost without warning. I most heartily rejoice when I hear of the advent of a "Tokology Baby."

Mrs. K. writes: "Send me an outfit for Tokology. My aunt in Dakota says, 'If you must sell books, sell Tokology, as it is, next to the Bible, the best book I ever read.'" Sample pages free. Agents wanted. Prepaid $2.75.

ALICE B. STOCKHAM & CO., 277 Madison St., Chicago.

THE KINDERGARTEN. A monthly magazine for home and school, science lessons, stories games, occupations, etc. Invaluable for primary teachers and mothers. Every home is made brighter and sweeter by the aids this magazine gives in the training of little children. $1.50 a year. On trial, 3 months, 30 cents.

ALICE B. STOCKHAM & CO., 277 Madison St., Chicago.

LEMON JELLY NO. 2.

Soak one box of gelatine in cold water an hour, then add one pint boiling water, two cups sugar, three lemons with skin and pulp. Let stand a while then strain through napkin into moulds.

COFFEE JELLY.

One and one half pints of nice, clear coffee, strong and hot, poured on one half box of gelatine, one cup of sugar, strain into a mould.

ORANGE BASKETS.

Orange baskets are just the things for children's parties and delight the little people. Trace the lines for the handle of the basket before cutting through the skin. Remove the pulp carefully and use it in making jelly. Keep the baskets in water or in a cool place until wanted, then fill with cubes of the jelly. To add to the effect squares of bright red jelly, like crabapple or current, may be mixed with the other, or a spoonful of whipped cream placed on top.

ROCK CREAM.

Boil one teacupful of good rice in sweet milk till soft. Sweeten it with powdered sugar and pile high on a dish. Lay on it here and there pieces of currant jelly or any kind of preserved fruit. Beat up very stiff the whites of three or four eggs and a little powdered sugar. Flavor with vanilla and drop over the rice, giving it the appearance of a rock of snow.

GRAHAM PUDDING.

One and one-half cups graham flour, one cup milk, one half cup molasses, one cup currants or raisins, one half teaspoon salt, one teaspoon soda. Sift the graham flour to make it light, dissolve soda in one tablespoon milk, add the remainder of the milk, salt and molasses; pour this mixture on the graham and beat well; add fruit which is floured a little; put in buttered mould and steam four hours. Serve with foamy sauce.

HORLICK'S

MALTED MILK

THE BEST FOOD FOR

Infants, Invalids, Dyspeptics, Convalescents, The Aged, Travelers and Nursing Mothers.

REQUIRES NO COOKING AND NO ADDITION OF MILK.
SIMPLY PREPARED BY DISSOLVING IN WATER.

A MOTHER'S GREATEST DESIRE is to see her child healthy, strong and well developed.

A BABY'S GREATEST NEED is a perfect food to keep pace with its rapid growth.

HORLICK'S MALTED MILK will satisfy these demands. Babies fed upon it grow into robust, healthy children. By its use most of the troubles incident to the summer season will be avoided.

RECOMMENDED BY PHYSICIANS.

For delicate ladies and for children it makes a most pleasant and nutritious table drink, either hot or iced, in place of tea and coffee.

For Sale by All Druggists.

A sample bottle will be sent free to any mother or invalid sending address to

MALTED MILK CO.,

SOLE MANUFACTURERS,

London, Eng.   Racine, Wis.

FOAMY SAUCE.

One half cup butter, one cup powdered sugar, one teaspoon vanilla, one fourth cup boiling water, white of one egg beaten to a froth. Cream the butter, add sugar gradually, then vanilla, and just before serving, add boiling water; stir well, then add egg and beat to a foam.

APPLE SNOW.

Three large tart apples, whites of three eggs, one half cup powdered sugar; pare, quarter and core the apples; steam until tender; strain and rub through fruit press; beat the whites of eggs stiff, add the sugar, one tablespoon at a time, beating stiff each time; add apples and beat again; pile lightly in glass dish and serve with

BOILED CUSTARD.

One pint milk, yolks of three eggs, three tablespoons sugar, one half teaspoon vanilla and a pinch of salt. Scald the milk in double boiler, add sugar and salt to eggs, then beat all together with a spoon, pour the hot milk slowly on this mixture. When well mixed pour back into boiler and cook until it thickens a little; then strain it and when nearly cold, add the flavoring.

ORANGE CHARLOTTE.

Soak one-third box gelatine in one-third cup of cold water until soft, then add one third cup boiling water; add cup of sugar and juice of one lemon; strain this and add one cup orange juice, pulp and little grated rind. Set in cool place and when beginning to harden, beat whites of three eggs stiff and beat into the jelly, beat all until stiff enough to drop from the spoon; pour into plain mould lined with sections of orange. Serve very cold with or without whipped cream.

CUSTARD SOUFFLE.

Make a sauce of one large tablespoon butter, two of flour, add a cup of milk; beat the yolks of four eggs, with two tablespoons sugar, add to the sauce and set away to cool. Half an hour before serving, beat the whites of four eggs stiff and cut them into this mixture lightly. Bake in buttered dish one half hour and serve immediately with creamy sauce.

CREAMY SAUCE.

Cream one-fourth cup butter, add gradually one half cup powdered sugar, then two tablespoons milk and flavoring. Heat over hot water and stir until smooth.

HARD SAUCE.

Two cups of powdered sugar, a piece of butter the size of an egg, about a teaspoonful of hot water to moisten the butter; beat well and keep in a cool place.

CHOCOLATE SAUCE.

One cup and a half of boiling water, one cup of sugar, one square of chocolate. Let the sugar and chocolate dissolve. Stir into the boiling water. Thicken with flour, add salt and flavor with vanilla.

CHOCOLATE CUSTARD.

Make same as Coffee custard, using one or two squares grated chocolate moistened with part of the milk.

APPLE DUMPLINGS.

One cup flour, one tablespoon lard, one-half tablespoon butter, one half teaspoon baking powder. Mix with milk until soft enough to handle; roll or pound out like pie crust; cut into round shapes, place three small quarters of apple on each, season with sugar and cinnamon, fold and bake; serve with

PLAIN PUDDING SAUCE.

One cup sugar, one-half cup butter, one large spoonful flour. Beat all together until white and smooth; pour on one pint boiling water; flavor with lemon extract.

COFFEE CUSTARD.

Boil one pint milk with one half cup sugar. Add one cup strong hot coffee and three beaten eggs; then one tablespoon corn starch dissolved in milk. Stir until smooth. Serve in cold glasses with meringue or whipped cream on top.

SUET PUDDING.

Four cups flour, one cup chopped raisins, three-fourths cup chopped suet, one cup half filled with molasses and filled up with sugar, one and one half cups sweet milk, one teaspoon soda, one teaspoon salt, steam three hours.

SAUCE FOR SUET PUDDING.

One cup of sugar and one egg and pinch of salt beaten well together. Just before serving boil one cup milk and pour over the sugar and egg, stirring well. Flavor with vanilla.

RICE CUSTARD.

Two-thirds of a cup of rice, steamed till quite soft in one quart of milk. Two-thirds cup sugar, one teaspoon salt, one teaspoon butter, when taken from the stove add the well beaten yolks of three eggs and one tablespoon of vanilla. Beat the whites of the three eggs stiff with three small tablespoons of sugar, added slowly. When stiff drop by spoonfuls on a plate and brown slightly in a hot oven and when the pudding is cold slip the frosting to the top of the pudding with a knife.

PINE APPLE-JELLY.

One-half box gelatine soaked in one cup water; add enough hot water to make a quart; add one cup sugar, juice of one can pine apple sliced, juice of three lemons. Strain into dish to cool. When it begins to thicken add pine-apple cut in small pieces; also candied cherries or sliced bananas. Serve with whipped cream if desired.

FRUIT BLANC-MANGE.

One and one-half pints hot water, one-half box gelatine dissolved in hot water, four tablespoons corn starch (quite rounding). Cook until the corn starch is well done, then turn in jam of any kind, stir well, and turn into mould. Serve cold with sweetened cream.

CHARLOTTE RUSSE.

Soak one-fourth box gelatine in one-fourth cup cold water until soft. Chill and whip one pint cream. Line a three pint mould with lady fingers. Sift one third cup sugar over the cream and add one teaspoon vanilla, Dissolve the gelatine in one-fourth cup boiling water and strain through fine strainer over cream; mix carefully and when nearly stiff enough to drop, pour into mould.

ICE CREAMS AND ICES.

NEW YORK ICE CREAM.

I_ _ __ _quart milk, beat together two eggs, one cup sugar, two tea
spoons of flour and one saltspoon salt. Add boiling milk and cook in
doub_ _oiler twenty minutes stirring until smooth, then occasionally.
Strain _d when cool add one quart of cream, flavoring and sugar to be
quite sw__ Freeze.

To Freeze.—Use one measure of coarse salt to three measures of ice
pounded fine, pack solidly and do not drain off water. A pint of nut
meats hickory or English walnuts, or one pound figs may be added to the
cream while freezing This will make about three quarts

ORANGE SHERBET.

_ _ _in_ sugar and one pint water, juice and pulp of six oranges.
Soak _ a _ _ble spoon gelatine in one-fourth cup of cold water and dissolve
with one _ourth cup boiling water. Strain and add to above mixture and
freeze. One can of grated pine-apple may be used same as oranges.

GLACE MERINGUE.

One quart cream, one large cup granulated sugar, one tablespoon vanilla, one cup milk one-fourth cup cold water in which is soaked one tablespoon gelatine; whites of six eggs, six tablespoons of powdered sugar. Let the milk come to a boil and stir in soaked gelatine. Strain into the cream, add vanilla and sugar and freeze. When frozen take out the beater and pack smoothly. Set away at least one half hour. When ready to serve, beat the whites of eggs stiff and gradually beat in the powdered sugar. Turn the frozen cream out on a plate and cover with meringue and brown. Serve immediately.

FROZEN FRUIT.

Cut up the contents one can peaches or apricots of course fresh fruit better, add one pint sugar, one quart water; freeze.

ICE CREAM.

One quart pure cream, sweeten with one cup sugar, one half vanilla, or one quart strawberries; crushed, strained and sweetened.

LUSCIOUS ICE CREAM.

One half pint can of **"Evaporated Cream,"** pint and a half one pint pure water, two cups sugar, flavor to taste and freeze.

www.ingramcontent.com/pod-product-compliance
Lightning Source LLC
Chambersburg PA
CBHW030552270326
41927CB00008B/1621